The Sex

Essays on Spirituality, Sexuality, & Restoration

Andrew J. Bauman

DEDICATION

To the courageous men who are willing to do the awkward and painful work of restoration, and to the countless number of women who have led the way.

ISBN: 9798691581175

Table of Contents

PART TWO: HEALING & WHOLENESS

ACKNOWLEDGMENTS

First, I want to thank my wife, Christy. She has taught me so much that is within this book. My dear, we have suffered together to learn these heartbreaking truths. Thank you for your love and your belief in my goodness; it has transformed me. May I continue to become the man you knew I was when we married. Thank you to my editor, Rose Gwynn, who labored over these words to make them something beautiful.

ENDORSEMENTS

"Most of us have some sense as to what God says about sex. Few of us have a sense of what sex says about God. In *The Sexually Healthy Man*, Andrew Bauman shows men how sexuality can be a window into understanding God more deeply; as well as understanding the glory and strength of our own masculine soul. With a rare blend of disarming vulnerability and trauma-informed clinical wisdom, Andrew lovingly helps readers understand the real nature of sexual brokenness. Best of all, he sets men on a proven path to living wholehearted and free in a way that will make us all think differently about sex, spirituality, and restoration."

Michael John Cusick, CEO at Restoring the Soul, Inc. Author of *Surfing for God*

"*The Sexually Healthy Man* arises out of the immense courage of therapist, Andrew Bauman. The title may seem like an oxymoron to any man paying attention to a newsfeed or a mirror. It's tempting to see the debris of sexual harm around us and within us and respond with despair or minimization. Andrew invites us to an alternative path that is both unflinchingly honest and hope restoring. This is a generous book, full of stories and wisdom. *The Sexually Healthy Man* can guide you to personal healing and, in the process, it might also enliven you to be a participant in the seismic cultural change needed in our world today."

Jay Stringer, M.Div, MA

Author of *Unwanted: How Sexual Brokenness Reveals Our Way to Healing*

"As a young therapist, I devoured Irvin Yalom's *The Gift of Therapy* - winsome and wise letters to his therapists and patients nudging them along in a journey of healing. Like Yalom's short letters,

Andrew's essays are deep but accessible, courageous, and compassionate, offered out of the experience of a seasoned therapist. They're engaging invitations to heal our systems and ourselves by addressing our stories, our bodies, and our fears of sex and sexuality. What a gift!"

Chuck DeGroat, PH.D.
Professor & Author
Senior Fellow, Newbigin House of Studies

"Andrew makes us look in the mirror and see how pornography delivers a fatal blow to our relationships and legacies. Demonstrating how porn shapes men's perceptions of sex and women, this book will open eyes and provide clarity to how this cancer is destroying generations of men. This is a must-read, not only for those struggling with pornography, but for the women they objectify."

Eddie Capparucci, Ph.D.
Author, *Going Deeper: How the Inner Child Impacts Your Sexual Addiction*

"Andrew Bauman's essays offer a path to sexual wholeness without the shame of purity culture or the shamelessness of popular culture. *The Sexually Healthy Man* invites men to honor the image of God in ourselves, in relationships with women, and in society as a whole. This book leads us through grief into greater wholeness as we suffer our stories, befriend our bodies, and oppose evil with courage and compassion."

Drew Boa, Author & Founder of HusbandMaterial.com

"As a blogger who often has to pick up the pieces from women betrayed by the men they loved, this book made me hope again! What would the world look like if men would humble themselves, be honest, and reclaim health and wholeness? Let Andrew Bauman lead you on the messy road toward healthy sexuality--and real intimacy between the sexes."

Sheila Wray Gregoire,
ToLoveHonorandVacuum.com,
Author of *The Good Girl's Guide to Great Sex*

INTRODUCTION

I walked into the building for a preview weekend at the Seattle School of Theology & Psychology over 13 years ago. This weekend was a time to explore the school and its offerings, as well as to complete multiple interviews to see if I was a good fit for the Counseling Psychology program. I had heard that this was the best place in the nation to do deep, rich soul work. The Seattle School had a reputation for being edgy and raw; it was the wild wild west of Christian graduate programs. Nevertheless, after the first preview day, I was thoroughly unimpressed. I figured I had already completed the work of dealing with the many betrayals of my father, as I had done plenty of counseling over the years. As I began to walk toward the academic counselor's office to express my disappointment, I heard a voice emanate from my gut. I couldn't determine if it was indigestion or the voice of God, but I heard it say, *Here is where you will address your sexuality.* The voice nearly stopped me in my tracks. I was suddenly terrified, and yet I knew immediately that this was the exact place I needed to be. And that proved to be the case.

As I sit here years later, I have dedicated my life to healing and restoring brokenness within male sexuality. I have by no means arrived at the pinnacle of sexual health, but living through a broken sexual story has taught me a lot. The message of this book is not a how-to or an opportunity to say, "Look how healed I am, now do what I did." No, this is a messy signpost, one where the wood is tired and worn, and you can just barely read what it says. Yes, this is a guide for me just as much as it is for you. I am thankful to God that I am no longer in active addiction to pornography; I have been sober for twelve years now. Yet, I know addiction is still in me, as I have been marked by both darkness and light. There is glory and depravity within me, and I have made peace with that fact.

Wherever you are on your healing journey, I am happy you have picked up this book. My goal in providing this shame-free resource is to advance the conversation around what sexual health means for men in Christian communities. It's time we begin to ask ourselves the difficult questions without shame or self-contempt, having the courage to become truly authentic and vulnerable with our sexuality and the stories we have written. This work is for each of us, no matter where we are or what we have done. There is hope, if you are willing to suffer and bleed for healing and wholeness.

So, what is a sexually healthy man? It's actually quite difficult to define. Everyone has their own story, culture, and beliefs that inform what they believe about sexuality.

The World Health Organization defines sexual health as:

A state of physical, emotional, mental, and social well-being in relation to sexuality... Sexual health requires a positive and respectful approach to sexuality and sexual relationships, as well as the possibility of having pleasurable and safe sexual experiences free of coercion, discrimination, and violence. For sexual health to be attained and maintained, the sexual rights of all persons must be respected, protected, and fulfilled.

This book will focus on the "state of physical, emotional, mental, and social well-being in relation to sexuality" from an evangelical perspective. I grew up in the Southern Baptist church of the 90's during the height of the True Love Waits movement and Joshua Harris' bestseller, *I Kissed Dating Goodbye*. (If you don't know what I am referring to, consider yourself blessed.) Many of the ideas espoused by these voices were infused with fear and shame, while giving no practical help or guidance in equipping us to become healthy sexual human beings. I became accustomed to feeling shame about sex, trying to white-knuckle purity, and yet somehow always falling short. The result was even more self-hatred. I needed more than that. Christian men need guidance and better resources for what it means to be sexually healthy, and Christian women need to know what attributes to look for and require from a partner.

This sexual healing journey can be an arduous one. Here are some practical steps and actions you can take as you enter into this work. First, find a trusted guide. This can be a therapist, a pastor, or a gentle-hearted friend, but it must be someone who has taken this path and gone before you, for they know that the terrain is not one without pain and heartache.

Second, find an authentic community to journey with you. If you are unable to find a local group, you can access incredible support groups around the world online. Connecting with others who have been through and know this journey is vital to your success in becoming a sexually healthy man.

Some foundational work you can do as you get into this book would be to write out a sexual timeline. Answer the following questions: Where were you first exposed to sexually explicit content? Was it kids at school; a cousin; a neighbor? What did your parents teach you (or not teach you) about pornography? What were you taught about sexual abuse? Who taught you about your body? About the body of a woman? Map out each event from birth to your current age to get an overview of where you have been, and where you are currently in regard to your sexuality. This timeline can serve as a backdrop to write more fully about any of these experiences.

Second, choose one of these events and write no less than a thousand words about it, bringing all five senses to the story and feeling it deeply within your own body. Whatever you can't remember, fill in the gaps with what you think probably happened. This is not going to be an exact photographic memory; rather, you are creating a piece of impressionistic art in an effort to evoke feeling and promote healing. Bring this deep-dive story to your therapist and/or guide. This process will be vital to your sexual healing as you enter into these essays about spirituality, sexuality, and restoration.

Thank you for taking the time and for having the courage to face your sexuality. If you take this process seriously, I have hope that you will experience transformation that leads to wholeness.

PART ONE

BROKENNESS

Pornocracy

How Porn Has Shaped Church & Democracy

Events in the news regarding sexual assault during the #MeToo movement tapped deep into the shame of men who feared being held accountable for horrific things they had done as teenagers. Women, too, feared they would be questioned and interrogated about the most painful and confusing trauma in their lives. I want to offer a somewhat different perspective on what I believe has played out on our national stage which, unfortunately, is far less hopeful.

The #MeToo movement began to shine light into previously ill-lit corners of our collective broken sexuality, exposing the ramifications of an entire generation of men's minds having been hijacked by pornography. This hijacking has created a pornographic mindset and style of relating in an entire generation of men, and I believe the exposure we are seeing is only the tip of the iceberg. The last 20+ years of internet pornography has set the stage for men in places of power to live out their sexual appetites and fantasies in real life, by creating an unconscious misogynistic mindset and cultivating a culture of systemic patriarchy in our churches and government. In this essay, I will discuss what it means to work toward the redemption of this pornified system, and begin to bring justice to the broken and insecure men who continue to perpetuate it.

The Barna group launched a nationwide study on pornography in 2016 called *The Porn Phenomenon*. They reported that "most pastors and youth pastors admit they have struggled with porn, either currently or in the past." Even our most sacred places, our churches, have become pornified. While fifty-six percent of women under the age of 25 seek out pornographic materials, eighty-one percent of teen and young adult men seek it out. Eight out of ten men between the ages of 18 and 30 view pornography at least monthly, according to the study.

This widespread consumption of porn, by men specifically, has led to a baseline of objectification toward women; a longing to conquer, possess, and devour beauty rather than to honor it. This objectification has led to a growing unconscious posture of misogyny toward women. The pornification of our society and our churches has impacted us in numerous ways, which we are sometimes hesitant to admit.

How has this pornification and sexualization impacted us?

1. **By perpetuating unconscious misogyny**

Misogyny is defined as the dislike of, contempt for, or ingrained prejudice against women. In her 2010 article, *From Pornography to Porno to Porn: How Porn Became the Norm*, Pamela Paul states, "Countless men have described to me how, while using pornography, they have lost the ability to relate to or be close to women ... They found the way they looked at women in real life warping to the pornographic fantasies they consumed on screen. Their daily interactions with women became pornified. Their relationships soured. They had trouble relating to women as individual human beings. They worried about the way they saw their daughters and girls their daughters' age."

When pornography becomes our primary teacher and guide in our sexual development, we learn certain ways of being. We relate to women the way we relate to porn. This is what I call a Pornographic Style of Relating (PSR). Many men develop a love/hate relationship with women as a result of the warping of their minds through pornography consumption.

Consider, for example, a pastor who is secretly involved with using pornography, holding deep shame because of his double life and lack of authenticity. He'll be predisposed primarily to one of two extreme responses. The first response would involve some or all of the following: inappropriately seducing women he is around, or making them feel adored, special, and incredibly cared for/loved. The other extreme could include: leaving the door open during one-on-one meetings, convincing himself that his actions are "above reproach," being overly guarded and closed off, shaming women in his congregation for wearing "inappropriate" clothing, becoming extremely legalistic, or holding contempt or hatred for women that bleeds into everyday interactions. He won't listen to feedback from women or allow their words to affect him; instead, he keeps women at arm's length. His unconscious thought is, "Women are a part of my shame. I hate my shame, therefore, I hate women." The pastor's hatred of his own unaddressed shame is projected outward onto the women in his life and congregation. This projection comes out in the form of contempt, misogyny, and disdain toward whatever triggers his unaddressed pain. How else has this pornification of society impacted us?

2. By creating a culture of systemic patriarchy

A 2002 Ryan J. Burns study of heterosexual male pornography users called *Male Internet Pornography Consumers' Perception of Women and Endorsement of Traditional Female Gender Roles* found that the more pornography the man consumed, the more likely he was to describe women in sexualized and stereotypically feminine ways, to approve of women in traditionally female occupations, and to value women more who are submissive and subordinate to men.

Porn sets us up to believe that women exist solely for our pleasure, and to service our needs.

This idea sets the table for a system of patriarchy. Patriarchy is "a system of society or government in which men hold the power and women are largely excluded from it." When misogyny is deeply entrenched into the male psyche, the natural next progression is the birth of patriarchy. Following the unconscious belief that women are "less than," men take their "rightful" places of power, using women as stepladders to success while ensuring that men retain the power. This dynamic is made possible by women's own internalized misogyny and sexism. Bearman, Korobov, and Thorne (2009) in their article "The Fabric of Internalized Sexism" define internalized sexism as "when women enact learned sexist behaviors upon themselves and other women."

This systemic patriarchy has bled into nearly every fiber of our culture. In the United States government, women hold just 83 of the 435 seats in the House of Representatives. In the Senate, women hold just 21 of the 100 seats.

It's not just in our government, in fact, I would argue that misogyny and patriarchy are even worse in our churches. The culture of systemic patriarchy has flourished within the walls of our houses of worship. Though women make up the majority of church congregations, the Barna group found that only "one of every eleven Protestant pastors is a woman." That means less than ten percent of pastors were women as of 2018. We silence women's voices, equally silencing God's, simply so that insecure men may retain power and control. That seems far too steep of a price to pay.

Where I grew up in the south, women were less-than. No one would have openly said that, but we all knew it. We were supposed to treat women with respect to their faces, but when it was just us guys, we could judge their bodies, belittle them, and make crude, humiliating jokes at their expense. We labeled it "guy talk" or locker room banter, or claimed that we were just joking to take the edge off of any lingering guilt. When I got into ministry as a youth and college pastor, the culture wasn't much different. Yes, the jokes were a little tamer, but the boys' club was still the boys' club, and women were not invited. After all, they didn't quite understand our divinely appointed leadership roles, and their voices were not simply discouraged--they weren't even considered relevant to the important work of God that we were doing.

Thirteen years ago, I moved to Seattle, Washington, as I was about to start my graduate school journey to become a psychotherapist. I was a youth pastor at the time, so I looked for a new gig in my new city. I found a well-paying youth pastor role and put my name into the national search. To my surprise, over the course of a few months, I was selected as a finalist to be considered for the position. It was the perfect opportunity; I could go to school full-time and do the youth pastor job basically in my sleep.

In my final interview with the board, they asked me to describe myself in three words. I quickly retorted, "A.D.D.!" They loved it. I had them rolling and eating out of the palm of my hand. I was a shoo-in for the job, until they asked me one final question: "Andrew, we see you have a lot of experience in the Southern Baptist church. Are you aware that we have a woman as a pastor? How do you personally feel about that?" I froze. I hadn't even thought of that being the case. A woman?!? I mean, I had heard of these things before, but it was like spotting an endangered Finless Porpoise or a Bengal Tiger–exotic and fairly unheard of in the church world I grew up in. "Um…" I stuttered, "Well, um… OK well, I know what the Bible says about that…" I tried to make another joke and sound cool with the whole idea when, truly, I was mortified. I had deeply internalized sexism. I could not believe that a woman could teach and pastor *me*, a red-blooded male. The entire tone of the interview changed at that moment, and the following day I withdrew my name from consideration for the position.

This embarrassing story is only a decade old, and I still cringe thinking about it. I know many other good-hearted, God-loving pastors who are unaware of their attitudes toward women, and of how their own internalized sexism impacts females in their ministries.

One of the best ways these good-hearted men in ministry, or any position of power, can thwart the process of internalized misogyny, is to begin listening to the stories of women.

A few years ago, the hashtag Things Only Christian Women Hear began trending on Twitter. Women shared true stories of things they had heard in church. "You can teach the women and children; you just can't teach the men." "You are an amazing leader!

You'd make an excellent pastor's wife someday!" "Women are too emotional to be leaders and pastors. It would never work." "She can't lead worship, because no one sings along when women are the lead singers, but backup is fine!" And finally, "Biblical womanhood can be defined by marriage and motherhood." I remember how, a few years ago, a prominent Seattle pastor called women "penis homes." Sadly, these stories are not isolated incidences, and those with power must be the ones who begin to change the script. How else has pornification and sexualization impacted us?

3. Pornography has normalized sexual abuse and silenced the female experience

In 2010, Mary Anne Layden, wrote "Pornography and Violence: A New Look at the Research" in a book called *The Social Costs of Pornography*. Her study looked at women who were victims of domestic or partner violence. Among those who had been raped,

73 percent stated that their partners had used pornography. Those who use porn normally engage in riskier and riskier behaviors in order to maintain their fix. This is how pornography works: you need more and more stimulus to get the same dopamine rush. The World Health Organization cites: "One in three women experience sexual or physical violence--most likely from their intimate partner." Intimate partner violence is difficult to convict in the court of law because of the secretive and intimate nature of the violence. So, how do we fix this? What can we do?

We must know our own stories.

Have you told the truth about your life, or are you still committed to minimizing your own darkness and degree of brokenness? Are you willing to look deeply at your own story and see how the pieces fit together? Knowing our stories means knowing our pain, and knowing our pain is the beginning of transforming it. Are you prepared to grieve your unmet needs and betrayals? As Richard Rohr states, "If we do not transform our pain, we will most assuredly transmit it."

We must own our sin and our sexual brokenness.

We must take responsibility for our internalized misogyny and patriarchy. To transform these heartbreaking cultural norms as Christians, we must lead with our brokenness, as Paul demonstrates in 1 Timothy 1:15: "Christ Jesus came into the world to save sinners, of whom I am the worst." Tiziana DellaRovere writes, "Men must take responsibility to change the violent and destructive aspects of patriarchy side by side with women. Whether you have violated women or not, you must commit yourself to transforming the misguided, patriarchal values and attitudes that you have internalized if you want a life founded on love and a society based on equality, compassion, and creative abundance."

I facilitated a workshop on addiction a few years ago, and as it was nearing a close, I fielded questions from the audience. Someone asked a question along the lines of, "Have you as a professional ever struggled with your own addictions?" I was presented with an opportunity to break my silence, to step out of hiding for the first time, with people I sensed would embrace me in the midst of my shame. From my experience with clients who had honored me by sharing their shame stories, I knew that inviting a safe person into my own areas of self-condemnation would be liberating and healing. With trepidation and hope, I admitted to a roomful of strangers that I had been addicted to internet pornography. I had previously never confessed my addiction out loud, except within the confines of therapy.

When the words left my lips, I nearly lifted my hands in an attempt to grab them and wrangle them back into my mouth. In a panic, I thought to myself,

What have I done? But I soon began to feel something else wash over me: a divine and holy kindness, like baptismal waters washing away my shame. Maybe that is what the Holy Spirit feels like. In a place where I had always held self-contempt, kindness snuck in without my permission. The shame lifted, and I was able to own my story publicly for the first time.

As I scanned the room, looking for expressions of judgment and disgust, I found none. What I did find were soft eyes full of tears and kindness locked onto mine. Their faces were gentle, their bodies leaning in toward mine, as I continued to share a condensed version of my addiction journey. Even though I had spent years in therapy engaging my shame and experiencing a modicum of healing, this terrifyingly sacred experience of self-disclosure turned out to be the most liberating of all, not only for me, but perhaps also for my listeners.

We must each speak our truth. Despite the darkness our stories hold, we know that God is truth, and the more we tell the truth of both our glory and our darkness, the more we can experience God. Men, make peace with your shame; admit that you have, at times, been abusive as you have been complicit in this oppressive system that has silenced a part of God's image. Women, you must make peace with your shame and self-contempt. It is not your fault or your body's fault if you were abused. Grief and rage are the holiest places you can step into in this fight against injustice.

As we tell our stories, we must be aware of how embodied our shame has become. What parts of your body bear the trauma and have been harmed? Will you allow those parts of your body to also tell their story?

We must no longer be passive bystanders.

Crass jokes about women in the kitchen, objectifying or sexualizing them to somehow be seen as cool or "one of the guys" is not acceptable. It's time for men to use their power and privilege to say "No." What if the next time you were a witness to sexism you simply said, "No, guys, that's not cool," or "I don't really find degrading women funny"?

We must build a comprehensive sex-positive ethic.

We must silence the shame guiding our rhetoric around sexuality, especially in the Christian world. We must begin to build a positive sex ethic that is not based on a negative posture towards sex. Sex is holy and stunning. The mishandling and harming of women is a consequence of our silence and shame towards sexuality.

We can change this.

HEY, MEN! TAKE RESPONSIBILITY

FOR SEXUALIZING WOMEN

One of the biggest ways men can begin to change the current trend of sexual assaults, sexual harassment, and a culture of sexualizing women, is by taking responsibility for their past, current, and future failures of this kind. I know this is a big ask, but it can be done. It is a difficult and humbling journey to take, and many men are frankly too cowardly to attempt it.

And yet, don't lose hope, women! I see the men I work with daily taking this journey, and it is gloriously beautiful and wildly gutsy. I see men owning their failures and weeping over the harm they have perpetrated against women.

Men are stepping into the fullness of their power and healthy anger against their own abusers, no longer allowing their unaddressed pain to continue to poison their interactions with others. There are good men out there, and I am honored to have a front row seat to their courage.

So, men, if you are looking to deepen your integrity and cease your sexualization of women, here are a few steps you can begin to incorporate into your life today.

1. Stop parting women out like used cars

"Hey dude, look at her ______!" Fill in the blank with all the idiotic, asinine things you have heard, or even said, in the past. This has been considered normal male behavior, and it must stop. To anatomize women to fit our pornographic fantasies is a posture of devour, not honor. She is a complete entity; a wonderfully complex woman full of glory and depravity, and for you to part her out like a used car is to curse the very face of God. Ask yourself, why do you dissect her so flippantly? What need are you trying to fill by acting this way? Is it unconscious? What if you became more aware of your actions and how you engage with women in your mind?

2. Stop denying your failures

You will not cease to exist if you admit you are wrong, or that you have been part of the problem. If you can own how you have failed women in the past and/or continue to do so, that is the first step toward moving beyond sexualization and its firstborn son, patriarchy. Tiziana DellaRovere says, "Men must take responsibility to change the violent and destructive aspects of patriarchy side by side with women. Whether you have violated women or not, you must commit yourself to transforming the misguided, patriarchal values and attitudes that you have internalized if you want a life founded on love and a society based on equality, compassion, and creative abundance."

3. No more bystanders to sexism

I am still learning to be more courageous when it comes to being a bystander in the presence of sexism. Last year at my tennis club, my coach commented on a woman's body and made a joke about two-dollar whores. I froze. I couldn't believe what I was hearing. I didn't laugh, and tried to change the subject, but I wish I had been braver at that moment. I eventually went to the director and reported the incident, but I could have been bolder when it mattered most.

The "boys' club" is a powerful force which keeps us silent and the culture of sexualization firmly intact. We must courageously speak up when we observe objectification of the feminine, which reduces the masculine to an adolescent animalistic archetype. I truly believe that toppling this narrative is men's responsibility to bear, since we are the ones who continue to uphold it.

4. Listen to women

Stop mansplaining and start listening. It's very possible that you are unaware of the hell that women suffer on a daily basis, simply because you are not a safe person for women to confide in. Humble yourself. Start listening to their pain–without answers, without defensiveness, and without trying to fix anything. Women are not broken, they just need to be heard; their pain understood. As men, we can be powerful advocates of women, rather than cowardly abusers who endorse their oppression.

I believe in you.

I believe in your goodness.

I believe in your ability to self-reflect.

To break down and let go.

To be humble.

To change.

To heal.

WHEN MEN RULE THE WORLD

Growing up in my white, Evangelical, deep South utopia, we all knew it was true: men ruled the world. My presidents: always men; my pastors: always men. Most CEOs, elected officials, and anyone I knew who had real power, authority, or influence, was a man like me. I wanted power, too. I genuinely wanted to make a difference in the world, and I believed that developing a domineering masculinity was the answer.

American culture taught me that women were sex symbols; they were subjects for my lust and objects to be taken advantage of, not honored. What I learned from the Church wasn't much different, it just looked more respectable on the surface. Sexism was just as present, objectification just as potent, but the subjugation of women was actually worse, because it was cloaked in "godliness." The Bible was used as a weapon to shoot down any who dared to confront the status quo. "God" had ordained women to be our servants, in both body and soul. No one would dare to question "God." This social structure serves us men well, so why would any of us with real power want to change it?

I learned that women exist to tend to the household, raise the kids, cook the meals, and clean up after me. My wife was to be a virtuous Proverbs 31 virgin, but also satisfy all of my sexual cravings. Another way to say this is that we were taught to want a "lady in the streets, but a freak in the bed" as Ludacris described in his iconic song "Nasty Girl."

Women were needed, but more as a necessary function than an equal. They served a vital role: loneliness prevention and sexual release. There was no mention of, or potential for, genuine intimacy or connection. In fact, I didn't even know that was a real thing in marriage. However, if you wanted sex, companionship, or to medicate feelings and avoid childhood trauma, women were the answer.

I remember a well-meaning pastor friend with whom I was on the staff of a church pulling me aside privately after meeting my powerful, goal-orientated girlfriend (now wife), Christy, for the first time. He sincerely wondered aloud, "But Andrew, don't you want more of a helpmate? You know, someone who will support *your* ministry?" His words meant she needed to be more focused on me and my goals and dreams, not her own. I wonder now, why did she need to be small so that I could be big? Are we men so fragile that we need women to stifle their glorious selves so that we can thrive?

Men's insecurity is so chronic that we make others, particularly women, smaller in our minds so that we can feel secure. Instead of dealing with our core sense of shame and fear, we project it on the women near us in an effort to avoid our own inner pain.

Women in the church today commonly feel like they are too much. Too many emotions, too much skin showing, too much anger if they get mad at an injustice; too sensitive if they speak up about a hurt. If they are too kind or friendly, they are accused of being flirtatious.

If women are able to break into the men's club of church leadership, they can't be too emotional or they will be accused of being weak; yet they can't be too stoic or they will be labeled the violent, dismissive term "bitchy." Women can't win; it's a man's world. This weighty burden that women bear is not only unfair, it's evil. And men must be the ones to begin to change these toxic norms.

Men have attempted to strip the image of God right out of a woman's face. Femininity is under attack by a kingdom of darkness, and many otherwise good-hearted men are unconsciously part of the problem.

What about you? In what ways are you unaware of your own systemic sexism? How are you unconsciously advancing oppression? How will you change your behavior toward women in your life and/or your ministry? We cannot allow the shame of realizing how we have mistreated and harmed women currently or in the past prevent us from making healthy changes. We must use our power and privilege to no longer be abusers, but advocates.

FUSING SEX & SOUL

She was a model: tall, blonde, slender, and attractive. Her poster hung from my dorm room wall. I went out of my way to tell guys who visited my dorm room, "Look who I'm dating when I'm at home." I stood tall and proud, the subject of envy from the other guys. Their jealousy made me beam.

She was body.

What I didn't mention was that the last time I had taken her out on a date, I literally wanted to be anywhere else other than with her. I was so bored, it was painful. She was quiet and timid, and we didn't share much in the way of common interests, such as speaking. I could not wait for the night to end, and yet that didn't stop me from flirting with her and continually trying to seduce her, getting physically close with my body as I moved further away with my heart.

She was soul.

But I only treated her as body. I had yet to integrate within myself the fusing of sex and soul, so I could not treat her, or anyone I dated, any differently. I was shallow and selfish.

Porn taught me how to relate that way; that sexuality and emotions, or my truest self, were completely separate. Women could have my body (if only in my fantasies), but they were to never access my heart or my soul, for these places were far too vulnerable. I could not deeply connect with them. The more beautiful the woman, the more prone I was to objectifying her and attempting to separate these two attributes, both outwardly (hanging a poster in my dorm room) and within myself. This resulted in making myself behave more like a machine or animal, killing authentic desire for intimacy and going numb with artificial means of connection.

When we engage in looking at pornography or other sexual practices of objectification, we have to turn off our connection to our body. We remove ourselves from what we are actually doing: the act of objectification, pornification, and degradation. We convince ourselves "all men do it" or "I am not hurting anyone" or worse, "If my wife was more sexually available to me, I wouldn't need to do this." We lie to ourselves in an attempt to hide from the shame of our poor choices, rather than facing our pain.

Another way we learn to bisect sex and soul is through triangulation, typically with a parent. For example, imagine growing up forced to act as a surrogate spouse for your emotionally anorexic mother. You are expected to fill the gaps of love where your father is absent or disengaged. You are there for her, listening to her pain, talking when she needs you.

She, in turn, is involved and present to some degree in your life, meeting many of your emotional needs. The emotional intimacy between you is extremely high; you even argue in a highly charged way, like spouses do. When this emotional intimacy is so intense, it creates a psychological split between your sexuality and your emotional core, because in healthy relationships, increased emotional intimacy correlates with increased sexual intimacy. (I write more about this in my book, *The Psychology of Porn.*) When increased sexual intimacy to match intense emotional intimacy is not an option, like in your relationship with your mother, you then seek out a high level of sexual intimacy with zero emotional intimacy to fill in the gap, i.e. pornography. Porn use is a perfect fit for an emotional incest survivor. When sex is separate from soul, sex is reduced to a commodity, which increases the chances of sexual violence and harm.

If you have experienced this triangulation with your parent/s, it is a major part of your psychosexual development and who you are today. If this dynamic remains unexamined in your own life, you will continue to reenact it in your current relationships. Sex and soul must be fully integrated for healthy sexuality to be attained.

LET ADDICTION REIGN

A Poem To My Father

1 Addiction

2 Addictions

3 Addictions

4

Dad, can you be addicted to anything more?

5 Addictions

6 Addictions

7 Addictions

8

Damn, Dad can't you get numb yet?

9 Addictions

10 Addictions

11 Addictions

12

Will you ever stop hating yourself?

I am convinced that what you are looking for is not inside that bottle.

What you seek is not in those 14 containers of pills on your bathroom counter.

You will not find it in the next fast-food burger you consume.

Or with the next lover who is with you in your room.

You must stop running from what is real; all these numbing agents do not heal. You must first begin to feel.

Yes, feel.

Feel the pain of all that you have lost, feel the price your choices have cost.

Look back and see, the little boy and now the scared man you have lost is me.

For once, look past yourself, and see your boy's bleeding heart,

It's about time to admit your part,

Yes, feel.

Feel your alcohol, drug, and sex addiction,

Feel the loneliness of your isolation and depression.

Feel your constant lies, feel your shrouded alibis,

Yes, feel.

Feel your bankruptcy, the emptiness of your fantasies.

Feel.

Does it hurt more than you thought it would?

Truth is a wolf and bites much harder than it should.

Feel.

Now, in that empty space, that throbbing place,

Dad, I want you to feel my grace.

I want you to see love and redemption in my face;

Yes, I will still be here longing for your embrace,

Wanting you to hold me, to delight, to laugh, to cry and see,

The beauty of what father and son could be.

No matter what you do or where you have gone, no matter the future or what you have done,

I want you to know, you will never be alone,

I will always be waiting for my prodigal father to come home.

⇞

Since writing this poem, my father has now passed away. It was quick and both unexpected and entirely expected. He was ready. I can't tell you the complexities of what I feel adding this poem to this book, but it feels vital, a part of his and mine own redemption story, to tell the truth in all its convolution. I loved (and still love) my father. His failures taught me to tell the truth, and remind me now of the gravity of not letting anything have mastery over your life. **Sex is too small of a god.**

GRIEVING A LOST SELF

I knew what had to be done; now I had to convince my body to carry out what my mind was telling me to do. It was about 9:00 p.m. when I reluctantly began gathering my belongings. I opened my pack and began filling it with my sleeping bag, a lighter, a few cigars, and a couple of pieces of fruit I had taken from the college cafeteria earlier that evening. I grabbed a few layers of warm clothing to compensate for the increasingly brisk fall air, and stuffed my leather journal and small Bible in the zipper compartment of my pack.

As I walked out the door, I took a photograph off my desk and placed it gently into my left jacket pocket. I knew this photo was going to play a significant role in the task for which I was summoned into the woods this night.

I threw my gear in the back of my Jeep Wrangler and sped for the mountains, which were only about a 4 1/2 minute drive from my dorm room. As I pulled into the empty gravel parking lot, I cut the engine and dimmed the headlights. The eerie sound of silence, a sound all its own, echoed in my head. This was the sound I needed, yet it was also that which most terrified me. It seemed as if the cold air had frozen the forest before me. The woods called to me; whispered for me to enter and to thaw my frozen heart. I gathered my supplies and began my trek up Lookout Mountain in Montreat, North Carolina, at 9:45 p.m.

Beads of cold sweat began collecting on my sideburns and a small pool of dread formed in the crevasse of my lower back. As I hiked madly and purposefully up the mountain, the forest's voice urged me to come, to hurry, and to finish this. An hour passed as I ascended the rocky ledge of the mountain.

When I reached the top, I gazed over the shadowy mountain ranges of Asheville, North Carolina, as I unpacked my gear. There were no sounds but my own deep breaths. The stars overhead and the distant lights of the city captured my vision.

I built a large fire and sat down beside it. Staring into its orange and blue flames, I knew it was time to do what I had come here for. I gingerly pulled the picture out of my jacket pocket and stared into its iconic image.

Tears began to well up in my eyes, remembering the moment. We were on the beach late one night, both so young and happy to finally be alone together. She rarely laughed so openly as was captured in that photo. I was carrying her on my back, both of our faces pressed into one another, her legs wrapped securely around my body. Our heads tilted back in radiant laughter. We were glowing.

I remembered her smell, her brown eyes that pierced my soul, the softness of her skin, her innocence that carried me into the divine, and her full lips that made me weak. I felt free and captured at the same time. She was my god. She was to be my wife. The more I stared at the picture the tighter I held onto it. I had come to this place, this mountain, to finally let go; to surrender a god. She had broken up with me a couple of months earlier after months of toxicity. I knew we needed to end things, but I just couldn't bring myself to feel that type of death. Now, I had no choice. Up until this moment, I had been too cowardly to let go, but here at this altar, I felt like Abraham being asked to sacrifice Isaac. My most precious gift had also become my most insidious prison, and yet I did not want to surrender it.

I began to mourn.

Each scream gradually grew in intensity and emotion. My tears could not be held in any longer, as they streamed down my face. My screams matured to moans. "Why? God, why? Why? Why?? Why did you rip her away from me? She was my only joy! The only thing that made me happy! Why, God? Answer me!" My thoughts quickly became accusatory toward God. Knowing that God is secure enough to handle my rage and brokenness, I continued, "How could you do this to your child? You are just like my earthly father: distant, weak, and absent. How can I trust a God who is so heartless, so merciless? Haven't I suffered enough?"

Releasing idols can be quite laborious.

My questions gave birth to wails. I tore my shirt off and began tearing hairs from my bare chest, my fingers grasping for something to make my pain tangible. I had never felt grief so deep in my bones. All I could do was scream and clutch my chest. My heart was shattering; no human words could be made out from the top of that mountain, only wails from the deepest part of my soul. I continued to kiss her face and weep bitterly. I missed her so much. I felt so lost without her.

I came to the realization that I had no self; no identity beyond her. I was not only grieving the loss of a relationship, but a complete loss of self. A beautiful woman makes a poor substitute for God.

Hours passed. A fierce battle had been waged on top of that mountain, and my entire body was exhausted from the fight. I gave up; surrendered. One finger at a time, I released my grip on the photo of us and placed it into the fire, still hoping God would intervene, that an angel would appear and say, "*Andrew, Andrew! Do not let go of her, for I see you are willing, and that is enough. I will provide another sacrifice, and reunite you both!*"

Instead, I heard only silence. As I watched our faces burn, I reluctantly surrendered my false god. I felt nauseated, yet I smiled slightly as I released the photo.

I felt depleted, yet strong at the same time. I continued to allow my tears to fall to the rocky soil as the fire grew dim. Then, I crawled slowly toward my sleeping bag and fell to the ground, spent with grief and loss.

When I awoke the next morning, my body was stiff from sleeping on a rock, yet my heart felt lighter. My prayers flowed more freely, I walked taller, and I even smiled on my hike back down the mountain. I knew I was going to be okay. Just the night before, I wasn't sure if I would make it out alive, and yet, because I had the courage to enter into the darkness of my crucifixion, I began to feel a small taste of resurrection. I honored and survived my grief.

This was one of my first steps in reclaiming my relationship to both God and myself some 16 years ago. It grieves me even now as I remember, and yet I bless that lost boy who was so desperately looking for someone to love and fill him. I am thankful for his tenacity to grieve boldly and to not give up. Grief truly is the doorway to God.

WELCOME HOME, GRIEF

Hello, Grief. Come into my house; make yourself comfortable. I trust you, as you are a relentless yet steady companion.

Come to the table. Yes, my friend, you are invited to eat. You may have the seat of honor, for though I do not love you, I respect you.

I no longer fear you. I have seen what you are capable of, yet I am still here, and I am even more powerful since you have left your mark.

Gorge yourself on my flesh, for I have made peace with pain, I have frolicked with my own death. When you have had your fill, you may go.

You are welcome to return, for I am now committed to being hospitable to you, Grief. I know I cannot stop you, though I tried for far too long. So I welcome you; I welcome you to my home.

It may seem odd to talk about grief in a book about healthy sexuality, yet I cannot think of a more important topic to address when seeking sexual health. There is much to grieve in the lives of men who have become unhealthy sexually: the loss of innocence, the betrayal of your body, the violence against yourself and the violence you have perpetrated against others.

Your cowardice, your lies, the suffering you have caused your wife and your family; fill in the blank. There is much to grieve.

We cannot let go of our unhealthy sexual patterns until we have adequately grieved them. As the poem above states, you must welcome grief in and make peace with the pain of your story. We cannot grieve what we hate; in other words, if you still have contempt toward yourself and your story, your ability to grieve may be blocked. Compulsive sexual behaviors are merely core wounds, normally from childhood, that have been sexualized to help soothe the pain. Kindness, not cruelty, is the only thing that can help heal the younger you. Hold that little boy close to your chest as you have the courage to welcome grief.

FACE TO FACE WITH A DYING GOD

Engaging Beauty & Arousal

I was attending a professional training group to improve my therapeutic skills when I was brought face to face with deep, lingering fear and shame around my past treatment of women and idolatry of beauty.

One of the exercises we were asked to do was to pair up with another attendee for uninterrupted eye contact, with our faces about twelve inches apart. We stared into our partner's eyes for minutes, which felt like hours. We were then asked to complete the following sentences without thinking, from our gut:

"I see in your eyes…"

"I feel shame when I…"

"My fear is that you will see in me…"

This therapeutic technique is called "sentence stems" and is a potent tool that quickly gets into our deepest shadow.

For this exercise, I was paired with a very attractive woman. Her piercing wide eyes immediately drew me in as my heart sped up. As I stared into this stranger's eyes, my thirteen years of pornography abuse flashed before me, along with my shame about how many women I had harmed when I was acting out of my Pornographic Style of Relating (PSR). This woman fit my arousal template (*Dr. Patrick Carnes defines an arousal template as "the total constellation of thoughts, images, behaviors, sounds, smells, sights, fantasies, and objects that arouse us sexually*") and, in the past, I would have attempted to objectify and devour her to feed my addiction and numb my unaddressed wounds.

I no longer wanted to engage with her beauty in a toxic or degrading way, but I also didn't want to ignore what was going on inside of me. In my experience, the more I try to push uncomfortable emotions away without properly acknowledging them, the more power they have to control me. I had previously only engaged beauty within two extremes: *indulge* or *ignore.* I needed to find a third way; a healthy way that did not consume or devour beauty, yet also didn't pretend that beauty doesn't exist or isn't arousing.

Up until that moment, I didn't realize how much internal work I still needed to do around this issue. Why did her beauty have so much power over me? I battled fantasies in my mind, peppered with thoughts of how much better my life would be if I was with her and not my wife. As sexual thoughts pervaded my brain, I attempted to let them go as quickly as they entered. This is embarrassing to admit, but that is how quick fantasy can enter our minds and derail reality, if we are not aware of its power. I wanted to run, but knew I needed to stay present with my fear, with my arousal, with her. She terrified me.

As I faced her, my stomach was in knots, and I felt like I needed to vomit. My shame was so close, mocking and taunting me from somewhere near my right shoulder. I was reminded again and again of my idolatry of beauty; how I unconsciously believed that a beautiful woman could save and rescue me from my heartache and childhood trauma. In that moment, I was not face to face with another human, but a dying god. I had worshipped at the altar of her feet for thirteen years, and unconsciously many years after the porn was gone. (*Fantasy structures of a pornographic mindset and PSR can stay in our brains long after the pornography use has stopped.)*

As I faced this woman, I knew little about her except what I could physically see, yet my fantasy had made her less human and filled in the gaps of my lack of knowledge. I felt the presence of the Evil one trying to steal, kill, and destroy (John 10:10); it whispered to me to return to a life I lived some 15 years ago. Yet, despite my palpable fear, I knew I was being invited into a potential holy moment of transformative healing if I could just hold onto courage. The moments of profound terror are often also the ones where God's mysteries are most real. If I could reject the siren call of fantasy and pursue truth, I could come face to face with God. God is truth, and the more we step into truth, the more we will know God.

What was true was that this woman I was staring at was beautiful. I do not need to feel shame for acknowledging her beauty, but what I do with beauty is the question. I must not dehumanize her through either extreme: engaging her as a god or as an object. I must honor her beauty, rather than debasing it through idolization or fantasy.

Arousal is normally a source of great shame for many, yet the response of being aroused by beauty is a stunning act created by God, calling us to the beauty of heaven. Pornography and other perversions of arousal have caused us to demonize something potentially glorious. ***Arousal is never the problem, but what you do with your arousal can be problematic.***

When arousal controls you, the problem is not the arousal itself; it's your choices. We must learn to enter into our fear of beauty with integrity, boundaries, and courage. We must bring what we most fear–for example, past sins of harming women–into the light, to break their controlling power over our lives.

When facing my deepest shame and terror, I had to answer my deepest question and greatest fear:

Am I a good man, despite the evils I have perpetrated?

These complex questions are typically the ones we most want to escape, but what if we decide to no longer judge them? What if we pay attention to these uncomfortable emotions and arousals? What if we could practice *being* with them, instead of attempting to annihilate them? What if we could stop naming them "good" or "bad," and simply see them as an opportunity? What if we were curious about their unexpected arrival? Is it possible that they are here to help cleanse us, teach us, and foster redemption and wholeness? What if we could bless, rather than curse, these emotions? Within this posture, no matter what comes up in us, we can give ourselves permission to work with, instead of against, our pain, moving through it and into healing. Nothing is so vile that Love cannot redeem it.

The next day, I knew I needed to process all that was happening in me with the group. Had I chosen to hide my shame, it would have blocked me from doing the work I needed to do for the remainder of the week. I began to stutter about the attraction and shame I was feeling, and all that was swirling inside of me from the previous eye-contact exercise. The therapist guided the woman and me to the middle of the group, and had us stare at each other again. This time, he asked me to tell her face-to-face what was happening inside of me. She was gracious and kind as my face turned red and I tripped over my sentences. Over the next few minutes, my shame lessened as I saw in her eyes that my courage was a gift. The therapist invited feedback from the group, and they echoed the same sentiment. The men were in awe of my courage and integrity, and the women felt honored and cared for. I was shown how my shame clouds my view of myself. Other people, especially the women, could see how hard I was working to honor and not devour, to be a different man than I used to be. The only thing holding me back from full liberation was my own harsh judgments against myself. My inner critic was quieted as I believed the words of my caring group members.

My own shame, self-contempt, and harsh judgments were the things that were actually holding me back from loving well. The sins of my past were no longer harming me, but how I was *mishandling* the sins of the past was. As Father Richard Rohr says, "We are not punished for our sins; we are punished by our sins." I continue to punish myself for my sin. It has nothing to do with God, and everything to do with my futile attempt to atone my sin.

On that day and into the following week, I was able to bless my courage and integrity. Even in low moments when self-contempt and shame reared their ugly heads, I was able to bless my goodness and not let Evil win. I walked out of the group with a new confidence.

Glory looks good on me.

PART TWO

HEALING & WHOLENESS

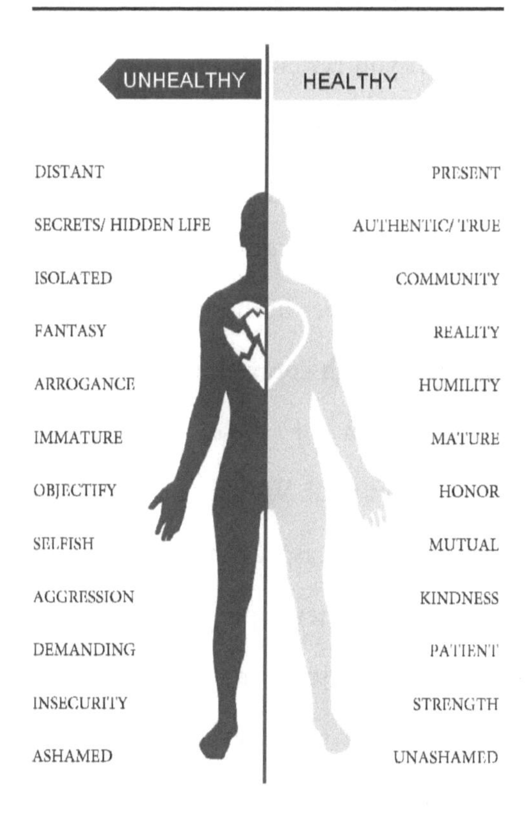
What is a Sexually Healthy Man?
UNHEALTHY
HEALTHY
DISTANT
PRESENT
SECRETS/ HIDDEN LIFE
AUTHENTIC/ TRUE
ISOLATED
COMMUNITY
FANTASY
REALITY
ARROGANCE
HUMILITY
IMMATURE
MATURE
OBJECTIFY
HONOR
SELFISH
MUTUAL
AGGRESSION
KINDNESS
DEMANDING
PATIENT
INSECURITY
STRENGTH
ASHAMED
UNASHAMED

WHAT IS A SEXUALLY HEALTHY MAN?

When you review the graph, what do you feel in your body? Do you feel regret, hope, or maybe a sense of longing or desire for something new? Where do you find yourself? Do you see yourself more on the unhealthy or the healthy side? If you have a partner, and enough courage, would you be willing to ask them which of these character traits they experience from you? Would you be willing to write about each of these aspects of unhealthy and healthy sexuality and how they apply to your life? Think about your past, your present, and what you hope for your future. Let's review these aspects of healthy and unhealthy sexuality together.

DISTANT vs. PRESENT

Simply put, does your partner have your face during intimacy? Are you with them, not just physically, but with the entirety of your being? Do you make eye contact during sex? Do you feel embodied, or do you at times feel you are a bystander to your own sex life?

SECRETS/HIDDEN LIFE vs. AUTHENTIC/TRUE

It is impossible to attain sexual health while you are living with secrets. Telling the truth is vital to genuine intimacy and lasting connection. If you are living a hidden life, the possibility for healthy sexuality is lost, because authenticity is the basis of trust and sexual health. What do you fear will happen if you allow your true self to emerge? You may feel terrified to be fully seen and loved, but that is what you truly need. This fear is normal, as many of us are not accustomed to genuine intimacy. It takes some time to get comfortable with vulnerability, but it is worth it.

FANTASY vs. REALITY

Pornography and other sexually compulsive behaviors feed off of a robust fantasy structure. Fantasy structure is a part of the system of arousal, yet living in unhealthy fantasy takes us away from our partners emotionally, making it impossible to connect with them deeply. As I explain in my book, *The Psychology of Porn*, "Fantasy is an escape from what is real. Whether it be difficult emotions, such as stress, anxiety, or depression, or just the pain that genuine relationship inevitably brings, fantasy relieves those struggles for a moment. While healthy relationships live in the truth, pornography helps bolster a life of fantasy that is difficult to undo. Fantasy brings relief but does not bring restoration." Do you live in full truth with your partner? Do you honor each other's scars and stories, or do you require them to attempt to become your porn-star fantasy, something that no human could ever attain?

ARROGANCE vs. HUMILITY

I have never met a sexually healthy, arrogant man. True sexual health comes at a cost, and normally that cost is some type of suffering which has produced an authentic humility. A sexually healthy man is humble in the way he gives and receives pleasure, attuned to his partner, and aware of both his glory and his depravity.

ISOLATION vs. COMMUNITY

Sexual dysfunction is bred in isolation. Most of the men I know don't masturbate to pornography in public. They do it quietly and shamefully, either at night when their spouse is asleep, or when they are alone in the bathroom. To be fully known, we must be in communion with others. Community doesn't just mean accountability, it means bleeding together; it means sharing our deepest shame, greatest fears, and deepest delights. True communion is fully knowing and being fully known by another.

IMMATURE vs. MATURE

Pornography use, secrets, half-truths, and lies are all examples of adolescent behavior. These habits indicate a need to look deeply within yourself and see your immaturity clearly. Ask yourself, "How old do I feel?" What would it mean for you to live into your true age? What parts of your trauma story have stunted your ability to become a mature man, and how can you give that part of yourself tenderness, kindness, and care?

SELFISH vs. MUTUAL

Pornography has taught generations of men to be selfish with their sexuality. In my thirteen years of use, it taught me that sex was about my pleasure, and no one else's. This conditioning is problematic when a real person is introduced in the context of an authentic sexual relationship, because sexuality up to that point has never involved shared mutuality. Mutual pleasure and mutual service means that both partners get to use their full voice of consent; they get to say "yes," "no," or "maybe" as they learn each other's bodies and desires.

DEMANDING vs. PATIENT

Building on the foundation of authentic mutuality, we must learn to be patient with each other as we grow in connectedness and listen to each other. Pornography and other forms of toxic, patriarchal masculinity have taught us that real men take what is "theirs." This has brought about a rise in rape culture and a normalization of male violence against women. Healthy sexuality is about consent and patience as each partner learns how to love more fully.

AGGRESSION vs. KINDNESS

One of the most obvious traits of a sexually healthy man is that of kindness. Kindness toward yourself overflows into kindness toward your partner. Sex is not about meeting pleasure demands or trying to cover your own insecurities by being aggressive. Sexual health requires stepping into deeply rooted masculine kindness that flows out of genuine strength.

INSECURITY vs. STRENGTH

The sexually unhealthy man is an insecure man. These wounded little boys try their hardest to appear big, because they feel so small inside. They try to find worth through money, toys, possessions, bullying, aggressive behavior, or the attractiveness of their spouse. These are all different ways of trying to overcompensate for how insecure they feel. Grounded, masculine strength never has to prove anything. Strong men know who they are and what they have to offer their partner and the world. Their strength protects and honors their partner, and does not try to gain mastery or power over them.

ASHAMED vs. UNASHAMED

Shame plagues many evangelical men. Some shame is guided by toxic beliefs about sexuality, and some of it is shame masquerading as guilt over living an inauthentic life. Shame and guilt are not the same. Shame says that the core of you is dirty and bad, while guilt speaks to your actions being bad, not your personhood. There is no place for shame in a sexually healthy man. He honors himself and his partner. He has made peace with his darkness and the stories of his past, and he now walks in courage and strength.

OBJECTIFY vs. HONOR

The objectification of women has become normative. Many times, through pornography use, men develop what I call a "pornographic style of relating" (this concept is explained more fully in my book, *The Psychology of Porn*) in which men learned how to relate to women from pornography. Sadly, pornography is centered on the objectification of women, making women "less" so that men can feel like they are "more." This view of women dehumanizes them, making it easier for men to harm them and more difficult for men to honor them. We must change the way we engage with beauty, standing in awe and honoring the feminine, which God created and named the summit of all of creation.

BRINGING YOUR BODY HOME

A Porn User's Guide To Embodiment

After a few years as a therapist, I realized that a strictly narrative-based approach toward counseling was limiting the depth of the work that I was able to do with my clients, especially those who were struggling with unwanted sexual behaviors. I decided to start training with a somatic therapist to step into healing within my own body, knowing I could not lead my clients to a place where I was unwilling to go myself.

During one of the first somatic groups in which I participated, I was quickly overtaken by continued grief over the loss of my son, Brave. The therapist guided me to lay on the floor. As the other folks in the group surrounded me, he talked me through a visualization of my son, as we talked and held onto each other. I wept bitterly and aggressively. He had the other participants hold me as I wept. As the therapist felt for trauma in my body, he found it in my belly. As he dug into my belly with strong hands, I wailed even louder. This healing of grief was different; it was embodied. I was able to bring my body to my grief in a new way, and this new level of vulnerability opened a door for me to allow others to care for the young and tender places within me that needed love. I knew I needed to bring this new way of engaging trauma and heartache back to my clients.

I see bodily disconnect in nearly all of the sexual abuse survivors and porn users that I work with. As a porn user for thirteen years myself, I had to split with my own body in order to participate in using pornography. If I told myself the truth–that I was contributing to sex trafficking, exploitation, and violence against women–it would have been much more difficult for me to achieve orgasm. Instead, I taught my body how to disconnect and to become numb to help facilitate my pattern of arousal. I learned to escape my own body. I spent years disconnecting from the truth of my body and finding ways to exist outside of myself. I believe liberation from unwanted sexual behaviors comes through bringing our bodies back home in a healthy, present relationship to themselves.

In his book *The Body Keeps the Score*, psychiatrist and researcher Bessel van der Kolk says,

"Traumatized people chronically feel unsafe inside their bodies: The past is alive in the form of gnawing interior discomfort. Their bodies are constantly bombarded by visceral warning signs, and, in an attempt to control these processes, they often become experts at ignoring their gut

feelings and in numbing awareness of what is played out inside. They learn to hide from themselves."

We must listen to the truth that our good bodies are softly whispering. Listening is a way to redeem the trauma of searing shame that our bodies have bravely endured.

So, what does this idea of bringing our bodies back home mean, in a practical sense? Pay attention: Are you aware of your breath? Can you feel the floor beneath your feet? What does your face feel like to your hands? Will you kindly hold your chest while you are anxious? Beginning the process of honoring and making a home in your body could mean thanking it for bearing all the heartache and trauma you have asked it to endure. When was the last time you thanked your good body for all that it has done for you? What about going to get a massage, or a long hug from a trusted friend and sojourner? There are many ways to come back into a healthy relationship with your body.

Listen to your body, for God resides there. Follow its leading.

Recently in my own healing work, I realized that I needed to continue to dig deeper into my own unconscious level of dysfunction with my body in relationship to touch, especially with women, whom I have historically sexualized. My parents were not very touchy-feely people. I knew they loved me, but touch wasn't necessarily a part of showing that love. By the time I reached puberty, the internet had become mainstream, and along with it, internet pornography. This exposure skewed my ability to make sense of healthy touch; all touch became sexualized in my mind.

Even after twelve years of sobriety and nearly eleven years of marriage, those broken places are still within me. Rather than holding contempt for these undeveloped parts, I decided to offer them care that directly involved my body. I started researching cuddle therapy, despite how strange it sounded. I knew I needed to address these wounds specifically with a mother figure. (It would not have been helpful or wise for me to seek out a young, attractive woman to cuddle with–that would have been foolish, and the opposite of what I was trying to accomplish.) I do not suggest this as the best approach for everyone, but I knew I needed to bodily engage in my healing process in a disarming way. I am too good at hiding behind my intellect and using my cognitive defenses, which keep me stuck in typical talk therapy. So, I went and cuddled with a very kind stranger. There were plenty of boundaries in place so that I felt safe, and it pushed me in such good and holy ways to make peace within my own body. Tears welled up in her eyes as I spoke of my issues with touch. She did not push toward places where I was too uncomfortable. It was beautifully uncomfortable and non-erotic. By engaging body and touch, a deep orphaned place within me received healing. This is just one of many ways that we can engage our bodies in the healing process.

What about you? How will you offer your body what it needs to heal? Our bodies are good and trusty guides. It is time we bring our bodies back home.

SEXUALITY IN THE EXTREMES

Shame vs. Shamelessness

"Getting off is getting off, it doesn't matter how," he said with a smirk. "I mean, I'm not gay, I just like busting a nut and don't care how it happens." My client's crude demeanor was no surprise, considering his unapologetic narcissism and complete shamelessness. I listened as he described his dilemma: he had received blow jobs from men in the bathroom of a local Walmart, and his wife had found out about it. She'd accused him of being gay. Somehow they thought "being gay" was the problem, rather than his betrayal of their marriage vows and completely warped ideas of sexuality.

When sexuality is engaged with in extremes, sacredness is lost. Sex becomes a commodity that is either indulged or avoided; on one side, rigidity replaces righteousness, and on the other, all boundaries and bodily wisdom are disregarded for cheap pleasure in the name of sexual liberation. Regardless of which extreme is chosen, intimacy and connection are forfeited for an unbalanced adherence to an ideal, which inevitably results in being bound by stronger chains.

In the conservative evangelical culture I grew up in, a sex-negative approach was their chosen method of sex (mis)education. Their ideology of sexuality was an attempt to avoid the complexities of the topic altogether, control and repress desire, and create an environment of fear and rigidity. Unfortunately, fear and shame are terrible motivators for healthy behavior and, much more often than not, create the exact opposite effect, making sexual commodification worse.

There is often great arousal found within the act of rebellion. What I have learned over the past decade of working with men and their sexual restoration is that neither shame nor shamelessness is the answer to sexual wholeness. Both extremes miss the point entirely.

The typical conservative approach, which tends to be more shame-based and sex-negative, has horrific consequences, as Tina Sellers notes:

"When people are filled with shame and self loathing, their affected self esteem takes precedence in interactions with others. It dominates and eclipses a person's ability to see and love another. In essence, sexuality encased in silence and shame keeps people from intimately knowing both God and each other and cripples our ability to truly love and be a healing force in a hurting world."

The other extreme, which I will address here as "shamelessness" has become popular in progressive circles recently. This approach to sexuality is a reactive counter-response to the toxic, shame-driven narrative promoted by more conservative ideologies. I am thinking of the stories I have heard from one of those "liberated" progressive seminaries, where a couple of the students decided to "mark" certain areas of the campus by having sexual intercourse there. This is not liberation, but a form of adolescent rebellion which stems from immense wounding and unaddressed heartache. Many of these folks take their painful stories and sprint toward the other extreme in pursuit of a radical escape from toxic shame, yet in that noble plight, they end up cheapening sex and making it less than a sacred act of love. Another example is the pro-porn progressives and therapists that I run into all the time. I believe they are well-intentioned, but merely focusing on shame reduction is to misunderstand healthy sexual reconstruction and wholeness. As relationship coach and anti-porn activist Jessica Bahr states,

"A therapist helping a client learn how to successfully navigate porn use is like a nutritionist helping a client navigate how to successfully eat fast food. 'Here, let me show you the 'right' way to use something toxic.' The problem is, changing your food palate AND your body after a poor diet (as hard as that is) is much easier than changing your sexual template/what your brain is wired to get aroused by. And, of course, it doesn't just affect the consumer, but his/her current and future partners. This misguidedness takes an important part of a love relationship, one that bonds and connects two people–physical intimacy–and replaces it with something so fake and so far removed from the person and his/her partner, so far removed from love and intimacy and actual mutual pleasure and desire, that it can't even be called a bad surrogate."

Shamelessness is no closer to healing than shame.

Pastor and theologian Nadia Bolz-Weber, whose work I have historically respected, has misconstrued sexual liberation in her new book *Shameless: A Sexual Reformation*. She says,

"I'm here to tell you: unless your sexual desires are for minors or animals, or your sexual choices are hurting you or those you love, those desires are not something you need to "struggle with." They are something to listen to, make decisions about, explore, perhaps have caution about. But struggle with? Fight against? Make enemies of? No."

Yes, we must make peace with our sexuality and no longer demonize it; with that I wholeheartedly agree. When we demonize sex, we set the stage for toxic religious shame. While I am against sexual shaming, Bolz-Weber loses me with the phrase "...unless your sexual desires are hurting you." You see, porn use *is* a direct way that we hurt ourselves. The Christian Post reports that in an interview with Out In Jersey, Bolz-Weber goes on to say, "There should be no shame in consuming pornography, especially if it is ethically sourced." Ethically sourced? Pornography capitalizes on the objectification and degradation of women by men, and attempts to call it ethical. Sure, some porn is worse than others, but that is not our standard. Our standard must be honoring the Imago Dei in the face of the other. Honor and objectification cannot co-exist.

Religious shame was undoubtedly a negative factor in my story of sexual development, but porn also damaged me because I developed a Pornographic Style of Relating (PSR), which made the way I related to women a nightmare for both them and me. Porn groomed me to seduce and consume beauty, rather than delight in and honor it. I was drawn to the quick highs of infatuation, rather than appreciating the slow and steady development of a long-lasting relationship.

Bolz-Weber adds the other caveat, "...unless your sexual desires are hurting those you love." Porn use perpetuates a false view of intimacy, impairing your ability to genuinely connect with those you love, which directly hurts them. Porn is also damaging for those you don't necessarily love–the women it helps continue to enslave, for example. The porn industry is driven by supply and demand; the more you use, creating a demand, the more the porn industry must supply. When you peruse the rape, incest, or 'young Asian women' categories, for example, these are the women who will be exploited and trafficked to supply your demand.

Our sexual ethic must not be based in extremes or either-ors; shameful and shameless are both terrible choices. We must learn to live in the tension of a middle ground that is grounded in honor of the Imago Dei; God in the face of all human beings.

So, what does living in this middle space of sexual health, where we no longer live into the extremes of either shame or shamelessness, look like? I believe more in-depth discussion is needed to flesh out what the process of healing requires.

PORNOGRAPHY SOFTWARE

Helpful or Not?

It's a question I hear often in the work I do with men recovering from unwanted sexual behaviors: "Is accountability software helpful or effective?" My answer, like most of the advice given in this field, is a nuanced one; yes, it is, and no, it isn't. Let me explain.

For each man who is at the beginning of his journey in becoming porn-free and learning to honor and not devour women, a few steps are vital. It's crucial to participate in weekly therapy with a sexuality specialist, go to a regular support group where you are truly authentic with the depravity and the glory of your sexuality, and, finally, be completely free of porn use to begin to give your brain time to heal as you dive into the root causes of your sexual brokenness.

That last step–becoming porn-free while you begin the healing process–is where this question of accountability software comes into play. I believe software can be very helpful during those first few months of learning to outgrow your dependence on porn. After you break an ankle, crutches provide a necessary respite for your wound to heal. But what happens if you continue to use crutches for years after your injury? What if you don't do physical therapy to strengthen and heal what was damaged? If you become overly dependent on crutches, your muscles begin to atrophy, resulting in the very thing that needs to grow stronger actually becoming weaker.

This is where accountability software falls short. At some point, you must address the pain beneath the porn. If you remain dependent on accountability software years into your recovery, are you actually free from porn? Do you have the strength to say no to the objectification of beauty on your own? How will you learn how to live differently? Will you enter your story of suffering and heal your core wounds? How will you know if you are a powerful man? How will you learn to respect yourself? The crutch of accountability software can actually tell us that we are weak, that we cannot be free of this prison. Only powerful men and women can muster the strength to break away from such entrapment.

I encourage my clients to take full responsibility for their poor choices. If they want to objectify, use, and abuse women, then that is their choice, and they should own it. If they want to cheat on their wives then I echo the great reformer, Martin Luther, by telling them to at least "sin boldly." Fully own that you are a misogynist who loves to abuse women! At least then, I can respect your integrity in owning your poor choices.

In contrast, most Christian men live hidden, split lives, parading as honorable Christian men while secretly degrading and objectifying others behind their computer screens. Continuing to use accountability software well into your healing process takes away your ability to own your sin fully. It delays what will likely be an eventual relapse. This crutch of software keeps us from outgrowing porn, as we remain adolescents by not taking responsibility for our own behavior. I urge you, men: own your failure, begin to make peace with your story of sexuality, and continue to grow in strength to live fully in truth and become the men of integrity that you wish to be.

A LETTER TO YOUR PARENTS

Reclaiming A Lost Voice

One exercise I often do with clients is to have them begin to tell the truth to their parents. This is not an attempt to blame their parents for their current problems, but rather, to reclaim a lost voice. We often relate to our parents in the same way as adults as we did when we were children. In some ways, we have failed to differentiate and mature in our relationship to them. Living into our true age rather than fusing with our inner child or allowing it to lead is a mark of maturity, and a sign that we've outgrown unhealthy behaviors.

Below is a courageous letter from a previous client who is reclaiming his lost voice. As you read, you will see it is not a letter of contempt, revenge, or venom, but a humble, authentic gift, inviting truth, intimacy, and connection. This is the ultimate goal. This type of authentic letter is not a form of dishonor, but immense honor and love. It's an invitation to genuine connection. It is important to remember that this type of letter is not so much for the recipient(s), but for you. The outcome should be change and growth in yourself, rather than an effort to change anyone else.

I hope this example will inspire you to embrace the challenge of reclaiming your own lost voice in your relationships.

Dear Mom & Dad,

There were some things we never talked about when I was a kid. One of them was sex.

Why didn't we talk about sex? I think you were afraid that talking about it would make me more curious about it, and predispose me towards engaging in premarital sex. This was the general fear of hyper-conservative Christianity: *Don't talk about it with your kids, don't follow that liberal agenda.*

I needed help in understanding my sexuality, but I didn't receive that help from you. I don't remember ever having the classic "birds and the bees" talk. I do remember one brief moment where you told me that "girls have holes." That's about it.

Of course, as a teenager in Christian circles, I heard messages about saving sex for marriage from youth group and school, but sex itself was rarely talked about. It was considered off-limits. The topic was taboo, and even curiosity about it was bad.

Surrounded by a hyper-sexual society, growing up in a family and social circles that viewed sex as taboo conversation, and hitting puberty and encountering my own sexuality for the first time created the perfect storm. When I needed guidance most, I was isolated. You weren't there for me, and I had to navigate that all by myself. Where were you?

My curiosity led me to seek out what women "really" looked like. I soaked up images of women in underwear ads, and eventually found my way to pornography. You caught me once, but after that, I learned how to hide it. I was already hiding the rest of me from you anyway, so it was no big deal to hide this, too.

My healthy young curiosity soon ramped up into a compulsive sexual behavior. Porn became my sex-ed teacher. This unwanted sexual behavior has plagued me since junior high, and I'm only now just beginning to unravel where, how, and why I got to this place.

You could have helped me back then. Maybe you were unable, scared, or unsure of how to approach the topic of sexuality. Still, I needed help, and more than just "Don't have sex before marriage" help. I needed my newfound desires to be treated as a natural part of growing up, to be normalized. I needed less secrecy about sexuality, about anatomy; about bodies. Maybe if sex hadn't been so scary and taboo (and therefore more appealing), I wouldn't be dealing with all of the consequences from my actions right now.

I made these choices, and by no means am I saying this is your fault, but it is important for me to name that you had a significant role in the development of my struggle. It was your silence and fear that enabled me to get to this place. I was just a kid, you know. I needed parental connection and guidance, not merely rules. I love you both, and I hope this letter can be the beginning of an authentic relationship between us.

LIFE AFTER PORN

Reconstructing A Healthy Sexuality After Pornography

Dear Andrew,

Before marriage, I was a sex addict who slept with hundreds of women and struggled terribly with porn. Porn was a struggle in the beginning of our marriage as well, but over time I have learned how to remove it from my life. I have never cheated on my wife, nor do I ever want to; however, a problem remains: I have no idea how to have sexual intimacy with her. I recognized that my lustful desires were sinful in nature, therefore, I have repressed them, effectively killing my sex drive. The thought of sex with my wife practically disgusts me–not because she is not beautiful, but because love and lust were two entirely different things in my mind. I objectified women for my selfish pleasure for years; I love my wife too much to do that to her. When we do have sex, I have to mentally take myself elsewhere to achieve an orgasm; I have to think of sinful things in order to meet her sexual needs.

Everyone warns about what porn can do, but no one seems to know how to fix the damage it has already caused. My wife says I look at her like a sister or a roommate, not as someone I sexually desire. She knows I love her, but also knows I don't lustfully desire her at all. I am glad everyone warns about the dangers of what porn can do to you, but no one talks about how to fix yourself or your marriage after the damage is done. How do I create good healthy sexual intimacy with my wife after sex and porn addiction? Is it possible?

Sadly, this letter I received is not a rare occurrence. This man's sorrowful realization regarding his sexuality is very common, but few men have the courage to admit they need help or seek solutions to remedy their history of broken sexuality.

A new generation of men is growing up in the grip of internet pornography, and consequently developing a pornographic style of relating and a pornographic mindset toward their world. An abundance of men are looking for a clear way to redeem their wayward sexuality after decades of porn use. Realizing that healthy relationships and unwanted sexual behaviors cannot co-exist, they are attempting to reconstruct a healthy sexuality within committed partnerships. Although these men see the importance of a healthy, mature sexual relationship that could last a lifetime, they are at a loss for what to *do* to transform their sexuality after the porn and other unwanted sexual behavior is gone.

Healthy sexual intimacy after compulsive sexual behaviors is possible; however, it requires courage, perseverance, and hard work. Here are some action items to get you on the path towards healthy sexuality:

1. Reconnect with your story

Our sexuality is never disconnected from our life's story. If you want to begin the healing process, you must begin story work. What is your story? How was sexuality handled in your household? Write out your memories and experiences around sexuality in explicit detail. What do you feel as you reenter the scene? Using your five senses, can you bring your body back into those moments? Can you humbly and kindly acknowledge the trauma without shaming yourself?

2. Tend to your wounds

Our sexual brokenness is always connected to the brokenness in our story. Whether you were the victim or the perpetrator, your objective is the same: reconnect with your wounds. If you can locate your wound, you can locate the doorway into your sexual healing. After locating the wound, what will you do to tend to it? Imagine your young son falling off his bicycle, scraping his knee. How would you care for him? Would you yell and curse? Would you use shame? Or would you kneel next to him and hold him closely? Will you love what has been bruised and bloodied? Will you bless, rather than curse the pain, the mistake? We must first honor ourselves through love before we can grieve our innocence lost. We can only grieve our wounds to the extent in which we love ourselves adequately.

3. Begin living authentically

Living authentically means fully living in truth. This is easier said than done. No more secrets, no more manipulation, no more hiding uncomfortable feelings. No more lies or duplicitous living. You are to be the same person at work, at home, at church, and behind the computer screen. It takes much more effort to wear and change masks than it does to live authentically. Once you are doing your story work and tending to the woundedness that drives your compulsive sexual behaviors, living authentically and with integrity will become your most obvious choice.

4. Practice healthy sex

You have spent decades with unhealthy pleasures; now it's time to practice healthy, intimate, present sex in all its glory.

First, admit your sexual struggles to your partner, knowing that they have little or nothing to do with her body or sexuality, but rather are a result of the brain damage that your pornography use has caused. When your partner has a clear picture of where you are in your journey, you will be more able to enter fully into emotional intimacy.

True intimacy is a foreign concept to porn users. When you have separated the body from the heart, it may take a while to realign. Be sure to educate yourself on your pornographic styles of relating to ensure that you are not unconsciously bringing them to your partner.

Here are some ways you can begin to engage in healthy sexuality and intimacy with your partner. Start with five minutes of uninterrupted eye contact. Sit a foot apart from your spouse and look into each other's eyes. No words, just lock eyes and hold the other's gaze. After the five minutes are up, talk about the experience. What did you see? How do you feel? After emotional connection is established, you can begin to explore connecting sexually.

Explore each others' bodies, communicating what brings each of you pleasure and what does not. Will you go slowly, practicing simply being with each other? Can you lay hands on each others' bodies and pray for each other? Each body part has a story to tell. Will you learn the stories of each body part and pray against Evil's accusations? Will you hold each other closely while naked? Will you and your partner hold eye contact while having intercourse?

The only way out of these damaging patterns that you have created is to fight for new healthy ones. I am reminded of Bruce Cockburn's 1984 song "Lovers In a Dangerous Time," when he sings, *"But nothing worth having comes without some kind of fight."* Will you fight for healthy sexuality with your partner and step into the uncomfortable space of genuine intimacy and connection? Will you suffer for beauty and wholeness?

New, healthy sexuality, not in isolation with your hand and the internet, but in relationship with your committed partner, requires much of you. Much heartache, brokenness, and pain. It will not be easy, but it will be worth it. Your sexuality can be restored and reclaimed into the beautiful, holy, and divine gift it was meant to be.

HELLO, GOOD PENIS

The Practice of Blessing Our Genitals

Our genitals are good. They were made for giving and receiving pleasure, creating new life, and experiencing radical divine joy.

Many times, our sexual organs get a bad rap; sometimes we even feel they have betrayed us. This often happens in the context of sexual abuse. Many victims of sexual abuse experience arousal or even pleasure in the midst of the abuse. This reality can be incredibly confusing, convincing victims that their genitals are the problem, marking them for life. Often, it is easier to place blame on our sexual organs than to feel the weight of betrayal by a perpetrator.

It is not our genitals that betray us, but usually a trusted friend or family member. (According to NAPCAN (2009), 95% of sexually abused children will be abused by someone they know and trust.)

Vaginas, vulvas, penises, and testicles are radically good, and God named them so at the beginning (Genesis 1:31). It's time we take back what Evil has tried to steal, kill, and destroy (John 10:10); to redeem what Evil meant to harm and God meant for good (Genesis 50:20). We begin this reclaiming of our bodies by actively blessing, rather than cursing them. So, what does this blessing look like? Below is an example from a client who had the courage to fight Evil through blessing.

"I have had a very dysfunctional and broken relationship with my penis. That is now going to change. I will no longer condemn and curse my penis, but will be intentional about blessing and courageously honoring my penis. My penis was given to me by a powerful, gracious God. I now repent of my disgust and cursing of my penis.

I honor the gift that it is to me. I celebrate the beauty that it is intended to bring to my life. I honor the joy and delight that it is intended to bring to my wife and me in our marriage. I am proud that I am a man and that I have this amazing gift that is intended for joy, delight, and honor. So, to my penis, I ask forgiveness for all these years of disgust, disdain, and hate. I choose to be proud of my penis and give myself full permission to enjoy the delight and pleasure that it was created to bring."

Let it be. May we all have the courage to bless what we have historically cursed in our story.

MALE EMBODIMENT

In my daily work with men, I have realized that they are innately disconnected from their own bodies in a way that is unique to their maleness. I am not saying all women are connected to their bodies, as trauma warps all bodily connections; however, girls grow into womanhood with their monthly cycles forcing them to attend to and be mindful of their blood and genitalia. As they age, many women choose to give birth, which is another powerful opportunity for women to become in touch with their bodies. By growing life inside their bodies and experiencing nausea, constant discomfort, and horrific pain, women are forced to confront their bodies in ways men aren't. There is also the reality of a woman's vagina literally being inside of her, whereas a man's penis is located outside of himself.

It seems men are comfortable with living disembodied. This is problematic, because our mental and spiritual health is dependent on our ability to connect with our own bodies. If God resides in our bodies (1 Corinthians 3:16-17), then connecting with our bodies is vital to connecting with the very God of the universe. If we as men remain disconnected from ourselves, how will we know true communion with God?

As men, we have very little that roots us into our bodies, except for the experience of pain. I think of God's curse towards Adam in Genesis 3:17, "Cursed is the ground because of you; through painful toil you will eat food from it all the days of your life" (NIV). It seems as if pain is the only thing that centers us in our bodies.

I am reminded of a time when I attempted the 2,173-mile hike through the Appalachian Trail. I was hiking over twenty miles a day, and the pounding and the wear and tear on my feet eventually caught up to me. I developed plantar fasciitis: little muscle tears throughout the bottoms of my feet, causing immense swelling. About every eight miles or so, the pain became unbearable and, using my hiking sticks as crutches, I would ice my feet in the cold mountain streams until the swelling eventually went down. I started popping pain medication with too much regularity in an attempt to numb what my body was screaming at me, and went on hiking for another month. Ultimately, the injury ended my ability to hike any further.

After over 900 miles, 300 of them spent limping and cussing, I went home. For the next five years, I could not walk barefoot without agony and a significant limp. I had not listened to or honored my body's cry for mercy. Rather, I allowed my insecurity to convince me that my ability to finish this hike was a representation of my masculinity.

Instead of facing my insecurities and listening to God's voice within my body, I chose cowardice while masquerading it as strength. I attempted to master my body and ignore its pain, and I paid deep consequences. The pain that my body was experiencing was an invitation to know my wounds and my God more fully. At that moment, I missed my body's invitation to the Divine, and only now, nearly fifteen years later, am I understanding the importance of being embodied.

What happens when we as men allow our insecurity to rule us, denying our bodies their truth? What happens when we stifle our pain, doing whatever it takes to silence our bodies' voices? It seems we have created a cultural norm of reducing pain at all costs, thus reducing our resilience and our ability to connect deeply with our true selves.

I am reminded of German Catholic Theologian Johannes Baptist Metz, who wrote, "Assent to God starts in our sincere assent to ourselves, just as sinful flight from God starts in our flight from ourselves." You must enter into your own body, becoming intimate with its voice, and follow God's lead.

Men, we must push beyond masculine socialization, becoming in tune with our bodies and God's holy and good spirit.

HOW TO HONOR YOUR PARENTS

One question that comes up often during the healing journey is, how do I honor my mother and father? Telling the truth of one's family of origin is vital to understanding the truth of one's life. To begin to live differently, we must first see clearly. Why does telling the truth feel dishonorable? How did being inauthentic become honorable? Shouldn't it be the other way around? If we are living fraudulently around our parents, what does that say about what we truly think of them? Doesn't living inauthentically in their presence show a lack of respect for them?

My young children often overhear their parents' intense conversations around death, the horrors of sexual abuse, racial injustice, or the declining state of our nation (yes, these are common topics in our household). When they ask us what we are talking about, we choose to dumb it down. We make it easy for them to bear; we tell so little of the truth that what they hear is barely true anymore. We do this to protect their little hearts and minds. It isn't much different than what we do with our parents, is it? We don't tell them anything difficult or painful to hear, because we know whatever difficult truth we present to them will not be handled well. We tell ourselves we're protecting them, but we're really protecting ourselves and our fragile fantasies of them. Our parents are grown-ups, not children, and in most cases, we do not need to protect them. Rather, we merely enable them to stay in their blindness when we choose not to bring the fullness of our truth.

Truth-telling takes practice, and is more of an art than a science. It's vital that we become securely differentiated from our parents in order to speak our truth to them. We also remember the wise saying,

"Don't cast your pearls before swine." If your parents are emotionally unsafe, you must be wise in your telling. Remember that you are not telling your truth for their sake, but for your own. I think, for example, of a young Christian man who recently disclosed that he was gay to his very conservative parents. He was terrified that they would reject him, so he had spent the last four years not being truly authentic with them, and as a result, their connection had dwindled. He had begun to struggle with mental illness, and was dealing with an increased desire for pornography and numbness. Whenever someone is hiding parts of who they are, genuine intimacy and connection become impossible.

Telling your truth is the best expression of honor you can give your parents.

Of course, there are plenty of dishonorable ways to tell the truth. Many times, truth is used as a crowbar to do violence, rather than a scalpel to promote healing and transformation. However, what I am advocating for is telling the fullness of truth rooted in kindness and love, not in arrogance or entitlement.

When one person in the family begins to tell the truth and step into their own healing journey, they begin to see the family system with new eyes. They begin to question the norms, and their mere presence is a stick in the spokes of the family system wheel. One person living in truth can feel incredibly threatening to others who depend on a toxic family system as a life force.

Breaking unhealthy family norms is honorable. In contrast, merely keeping the peace at the cost of your integrity is not only dishonorable, it is cowardice. Familial peace is not actual peace if it is built on inauthenticity. When we are living in truth, we live in full alignment. Our inner world and our external world line up. There is no splitting of who we are, no matter whose presence we are in.

What about you? Are you living in truth and authenticity? Are there certain people you remain hidden with? If so, what does that say about the power they hold over you? Is it time to tell the truth to your parents, no matter how poorly they may respond?

SEXUALIZING OUR SORROW

To break free from our unwanted compulsive behaviors, we must have the courage to delve deeper into our woundedness and explore what lies beneath it. We must begin to kindly, yet decisively, cut out the roots of our sexual acting out. To do this, we must first gain an understanding of how we are prone to sexualizing our heartbreak in an effort to bring comfort to our trauma and pain.

A client, we'll call him Sam, had been heroically facing the dark shadows of his past out-of-control sexual behaviors for some time. He had finally been completely truthful with his wife and his family about his struggles. After seven months of not sexually acting out, Sam agreed to sit down and speak with his mother. She had previously expressed her desire to have a more open and authentic relationship with him. She explained that she wanted to be a "safe place" for Sam to talk through his pain. The invitation sounded nice, but Sam had done enough emotional work to be able to discern that this invitation might not be as innocent as it sounded, and could come at a deep cost to his own health and heart. Sam desired to be closer to his mother, but in the context of love, honor, and respect—not to be devoured or treated as her surrogate spouse.

Nevertheless, Sam decided to give her the benefit of the doubt, and began to share more in-depth about the latest months of his healing journey. As he spoke, he noticed his mother becoming increasingly tense and agitated. The tempo of her questions quickened, and her curiosity dissipated as palpable anxiety took its place. It began to feel like her questions were more for her sake than his. When he realized what was happening, Sam shifted from sharing his heart and vulnerability about his journey to inquiring more about his mother and her life. It became abundantly clear that she, once again, expected him to care for her. Their talk about Sam's heroic journey had simply been the means to her own ends; they were really there to talk about her.

Sadly, this dynamic wasn't new; it had played out in their relationship for Sam's entire life. He always longed to be truly seen by his mother; for there to be enough space in the relationship for him to not be okay. He struggled under the burden of taking care of her emotions; what he needed was for her to be differentiated enough for her emotional world not to be tied up in his. Their enmeshed style of relating was what had propelled him into sexually compulsive behaviors.

When emotional enmeshment, also known as triangulation or emotional incest, is present—especially from mother to son—an unconscious longing for full consummation takes place. This isn't as outlandish as it sounds, and here's why. In enmeshed mother-son relationships, our mothers overtake all of our emotional needs but not our sexual needs. If my mother fills me emotionally, the logical result is that I seek something to complete the missing piece: my sexual needs. Since I am already filled emotionally, I have no other space for anything even remotely emotional, so I will seek a source of sexual fulfillment with minimal emotional ties or commitment. Pornography and other emotionless, compulsive sexual behaviors become the perfect solution to an otherwise daunting problem. I can feel whole (even though I am completely fractured) because through those two relationships—porn and mother—I can feel normal again. I am filled both sexually and emotionally.

So, back to Sam and his mother. A reenactment was taking place which could have been a real trap for

Sam. On one hand, he desperately desired healthy love and support from his mother during an incredibly difficult season, yet because of his mother's lack of emotional awareness and unconscious attempts at healing her wounds through her son, Sam had to withdraw from the current dynamic. There was no way that he would ever be enough to fill her broken places.

For him to continue on his path toward sexual health, he must continue to hold firm to his boundaries in his relationship with her. The alternative is that he will be emotionally devoured by her, and becoming more prone to act out again in an effort to soothe himself. He can show care to his mother, but care looks like directing her to other resources outside of himself, like a good therapist, a support group, or a trusted friend.

It's no surprise that later that night, after the conversation with his mother, Sam drank more alcohol than normal, and began to feel a sexual desire for exhibitionism that he had never felt before. Exhibitionism is the act of exposing one's genitals in public—in an effort to be seen. This is a perfect example of sexualizing sorrow. Sam was unconsciously heartbroken that, once again, his mother had invited him into the potential of being seen, only to completely miss him and make it all about her. His sorrow and longing to be seen by his mother then became sexualized, creating a desire to expose himself in public. This has nothing to do with his depravity, and everything to do with the sexualizing of his sorrow.

Sam's path forward is to grieve the fact that he has never been able to be fully himself in his mother's presence, and that he has never been fully loved, cared for, or seen by his insecure and wounded mother. He must differentiate from his mother, and continue to be rooted and centered in his deep goodness. If Sam can refrain from judging his sexual urge for exhibitionism and remain curious about it, he can begin to uncover the roots of his wounding and sorrow, boldly grieve, and remove the fuel that powers his compulsive sexual behaviors.

SHAME & NAVIGATING STORY

Healing your shame starts with examining your story. We must face our stories boldly, no matter how old they, or we, are. It's important to note that we cannot change the facts of our stories (and that is never the goal), but when we engage from a place of curiosity about the characters, themes, scenes, and particulars of our stories, we can change the meaning they hold for us. Through the work of story commitment, we can change the themes to which we are most loyal. When you face the shame that has bound you, you are staring into the face of the Evil one and saying "Hell, no!" No more, will Evil shame you for things that Jesus died on the cross for. As you do this, you may be surprised to realize that you have actually become quite comfortable with your shame. It can be difficult to release our shame, for it can sometimes feel like home.

Some of my most shameful stories happened in a two-and-a-half year period between my senior year of high school and my sophomore year of college. At that point in time, although I was a Christian, I had never addressed the pain in my story. During my junior year of high school, I had a spiritual experience at summer camp and gave my life to Christ (again). This time felt real; I even broke all my secular CDs (I still miss Bone Thugs-n-Harmony). I also joined the Fellowship of Christian Athletes (FCA), started a Bible study, and began preaching at my youth group. My life had changed, but unaddressed woundedness will always catch up to you, no matter how many CDs you break. Jesus was interested in the transformation of my heart, not just my behavior.

By the time my senior year came along, I was the student body president, president of the FCA, and captain of my soccer team, but I was also secretly addicted to porn and using women to fulfill my sexual desires. I was teaching and preaching twice a week, while also making out with different girls every week. I was trying so hard to fix something broken inside of me. First I tried Jesus, then I tried women. Neither worked the way I had hoped. Jesus wanted something I couldn't give Him: a heart. I was merely a shell without a story.

Thankfully, my life was changed by force. It was the summer of '02. I was 19 years old, just coming out of my first full year of college-- and nearly flunking out. A few weeks earlier, I had checked myself into the psychiatric ward at Pardee Hospital after holding a gun in my hand and considering whether to end my life. I no longer wanted to live, and I was too scared to be alone, for fear of what I might do. My Prozac doses made me sufficiently numb as I walked around zombie-like looking for life, love, something to numb my pain, make me feel joy, or anything that could make me come alive again. Over time, after everything had died within me and I had no other idols left, I began my genuine journey of healing my core wounding. With a trusted therapist and guide, I started letting my story, my grief, my pain, and my abuse matter. I started giving airtime to my story, and the more truth I told, the more I grew in kindness toward myself and my heartache.

STORY WORK

I would like to invite you to bravely face your own story and find healing. Here are some prompts to help get you started on healing your shame story.

1. Write a detailed timeline of your sexual development. This is like a map to locate where you have been. Start at the beginning. How was sexuality introduced to you? How was sexuality talked about, or not talked about, in your home? When was the first time you

were introduced to pornography? Did you experience sexual abuse? These events are like trail markers to help locate you in your current reality.

2. Choose one story from the assignment above and dive deep into that experience, using all five senses to remember the scene of abuse, first exposure to pornography, or sexual betrayal for example. What were the smells, the sights; what did the chair or bed feel like? What was the taste in your mouth? During this assignment, you are landing the plane into your story of sexuality, not merely flying over it. You must feel the weight of the story. If you decide to distance yourself from it, you will not get the full benefit of this exercise. Allow your body to enter back into what it has been trying to escape all these years. Write, bleed, and grieve this story. Then, bring it to a trusted

therapist or a friend who is well-acquainted with suffering.

STORY EXAMPLE

Here is an example of the above story exercise from my own life. I hope that by reading my story, you can learn how to be a better listener of trauma. This will help you to develop deeper intimacy with those you are in a relationship with; my story is a model of what writing your own story can look like.

It had been five years since my parents separated and we moved away from my father. He continued to live in Florida, while my mom took my two siblings and me to live near her parents in the mountains of North Carolina.

My father would visit a couple times a year. I had little knowledge of why we had left him, but my excitement was tangible each time he came to visit. He came bearing exciting gifts, and with each visit he would take me to get ice cream and new clothes from the mall.

I would always brag to my middle school buddies, Josh and Jordan, about how strong my dad was, as he was a bodybuilder, and how smart he was, because he had his own law firm and was vice president of a Christian college. I would tell my friends of his wealth, especially about how I got to ride in his new Mazda 626 with a sunroof. I did not know my father very well, but in my 13-year-old mind, he was larger than life.

One spring day, he picked me up from school. I remember how excited I was to show my friends his car as he drove into the carpool line. I beamed with pride as he pulled up, eagerly jumping into the front seat next to him. "How was school, Buddy?" he asked. "Good, Dad. What are we doing this weekend?" We continued the conversation as we drove away from the school, discussing our plans to go visit waterfalls and hit up the local driving range.

As we turned right from Highway 191 into our Dellwood neighborhood and began driving up the mountain to my mom's house, my dad began rubbing my back. I felt odd at first, as his hand went underneath my shirt. I quickly dismissed my discomfort, telling myself that he was my dad after all, and was just showing me love that I had been missing for many years. It felt nice to be touched and loved by a father whom I rarely got to see.

His fingers caressed my spine as we continued to talk about the upcoming weekend. Then, within a few seconds, everything shifted. His hand went lower onto the small of my back, and my skin began to itch. His hand continued quickly down my back beneath the waistline of my shorts. In an instant, I quickly lurched forward with discomfort and disapproval, and he hastily moved his hand away.

I immediately began trying to make sense of what just happened. It had all happened so fast. The next few minutes were a haze in my mind. Should I ask him what he was doing or why he did that, I wondered?

Should I change the topic of conversation? I do not remember the details.

What I do remember was that this moment was never talked about, never mentioned to anyone. We just went on our way as if nothing had ever happened. I remember having a strong realization that day in the front seat of my dad's car that he was a man that I could no longer trust.

I was not safe to be alone in my hero's presence.

STORY REVIEW

Check in with your body as you read my story. What do you feel? What did my story invoke in you? Sadness, rage, horror? Did it trigger some of your own unaddressed trauma? If you were in the room listening to me tell you this story, how would you respond? Would you attempt to fix me or give me answers to unanswerable questions? Would you say thank you and bless me for my courage? How would you want to engage my story? We usually engage others' stories in the same way we engage our own. If you are calloused to the wounds of your youth, you will be calloused to mine.

After you check in with your body, what emotion do you feel most present? Name that emotion. Let's say it is rage, and ask yourself if the rage is for my sake as the storyteller, or for your own sake as the potentially triggered listener. Is your rage for the betrayed little boy in me or your own wounded younger self? How do you offer that rage for my sake, and later tend to your own wounds that may have been triggered? One possible reply would be, "I am struck by the rage I have at your father for betraying your young heart of longing." This type of response is more meaningful than just a "thank you" or "I will pray for you." It is not a dismissal of my pain, or projection of your own unprocessed trauma onto me. Rather, this is you engaging my story deeply and helping me feel more connected to the loss and pain, and crucifixion, in order that I may also taste the freedom of healing, and resurrection. Now, this story will no longer rule me from the shadows. You can offer a healing presence that neither hides or indulges my story. Your empathetic presence can be a helpful agent of change and healing.

Are you ready to step into your own darkness and glory? Once you come face to face with all that you fear, Evil no longer has a foothold. Soul ties are broken, and rich healing can be found. May you have the courage to face what you have long feared within yourself.

CONCLUSION

You have made it this far, and that is something to celebrate. You are committed to becoming a better lover and having integrity in the way you choose to live by acknowledging how much pornography and the objectification of women has mastered you, grieving that loss with kindness, and saying farewell to your adolescent behaviors.

Compulsive sexual behavior is a cruel master. God wants you to step into the power of your authentic masculine strength; to live respectfully and soulfully from a secure center, dealing with your core wounds that unconsciously have directed much for your life. You can become an advocate for women, rather than a man who perpetrates their subjugation and abuse to soothe your insecurities.

It is time to take back what has been stolen and step into your glory. God, the creator of the universe, the sacrificial lover who demonstrated that love by sending his Son, Jesus Christ, to die for your infidelity and cowardice, is awaiting your return with kindness and care. I look forward to fighting alongside you in hopes of blazing the trail for a bold new masculinity.

I leave you with this quote from Nayyirah Waheed in her book, *Salt* (2013). This is my prayer for you.

> "i want more 'men'
> with flowers falling from their skin.
> more water in their eyes.
> more tremble in their bodies.
> more women in their hearts
> than on their hands.
> more softness in their height.
> more honesty in their voice.
> more wonder.
> more humility in their feet."

Made in United States
Troutdale, OR
01/09/2025

27790056R00098